Bourgeois Babes, Bossy Wives, and Bobby Haircuts

A Case for Gender Equality in Ministry

D1282839

Michael F. Bird

Bourgeois Babes, Bossy Wives, and Bobby Haircuts

Fresh Perspectives on Women in Ministry

Bourgeois Babes, Bossy Wives, and Bobby Haircuts

A Case for Gender Equality in Ministry

Michael F. Bird

ZONDERVAN

Bourgeois Babes, Bossy Wives, and Bobby Haircuts
Copyright © 2012 by Michael F. Bird

This title is available as a Zondervan ebook.
Visit www.zondervan.com/ebooks.

Requests for information should be addressed to:
Zondervan, 3900 *Sparks Drive SE, Grand Rapids, Michigan 49546*

Library of Congress Cataloging-in-Publication Data

Bird, Michael F.
      Bourgeois babes, bossy wives, and bobby haircuts : a case for gender
equality in ministry / Michael F. Bird.
          pages cm. — (Fresh Perspectives on Women in Ministry)
      ISBN 978-0-310-51926-3
          1. Women clergy. 2. Women in church work. 3. Sex discrimination.
      4. Women's rights—Religious aspects—Christianity. I. Title.
      BV676.B57 2014
      261'.14082—dc23   2014004492

Cover design: Ron Huizinga
Interior design and composition: Greg Johnson, Textbook Perfect

Printed in the United States

14 15 16 17 18 19 20 /CHM/ 19 18 17 16 15 14 13 12 11 10 9 8 7 6 5 4 3 2 1

For Ben Witherington III
who has done much to advance the gospel by advancing
the ministry of women for the gospel.

Contents

Abbreviations

BDAG   Bauer, Walter, and Frederick Danker, *A Greek English Lexicon of the New Testament and Other Christian Literature* (Chicago: University of Chicago Press, 2000)

BECNT   Baker Exegetical Commentary on the New Testament

CBQ   *Catholic Biblical Quarterly*

ESV   English Standard Version

EvQ   *Evangelical Quarterly*

ICC   International Critical Commentary

JB   Jerusalem Bible

JETS   *Journal of the Evangelical Theological Society*

JSNT   *Journal for the Study of the New Testament*

NCBC   New Century Bible Commentary

NCCS   New Covenant Commentary Series

NICNT   New International Commentary on the New Testament

NIGTC   New International Greek Testament Commentary

NIV   New International Version

NIVAC   NIV Application Commentary

NRSV   New Revised Standard Version

PNTC   Pillar New Testament Commentary

WBC   Word Biblical Commentary

Introduction

Many years ago the Baptist fundamentalist John R. Rice published a polemical booklet called *Bobbed Hair, Bossy Wives, and Women Preachers*, written to censure women for rebellious acts like cutting their hair. In fact, a woman cutting her hair was so rebellious that even the angels might be led into rebellion against God by imitating her example (yes, Rice actually said that!). For Rice, a worst-case scenario was probably something like a woman wearing pants with a Jacqueline Kennedy-style bobbed haircut, speaking from a pulpit, while her husband minded the kids in the nursery.[1]

Stanley E. Gundry has mentioned how Rice's booklet was important to his Baptist minister father, who harangued women in his congregation for outlandish behavior such as sharing unwanted opinions. Though Stan was raised a staunch patriarchalist, he was also instilled with a deep reverence for the truth of the Bible. Eventually he came to believe that the truth of the Bible permitted a place for women in pastoral ministry. Stan came to this view largely through the exegetical prodding and theological questioning of his wife, Patricia Gundry. Patricia in fact went on to write the book *Women Be Free!* an early evangelical manifesto for Christian egalitarianism.[2] Stan was drawn to the egalitarian position because he came to believe that the climax of redemptive history would bring about the restoration of male-female relationships as evidenced in creation, that patriarchalists seek to prohibit women from doing the very things we see women doing in the Bible, and that advocates for patriarchal hierarchalism would one day be viewed as derisively as we now view Christian defenders of slavery in the nineteenth century.[3]

Stan's story is not unique, as many devout evangelical men and women of faith have had something of an epiphany on women and leadership that moved them toward a more inclusive view of ministry.[4] I share in that story. Admittedly, I would demur with Stan and other egalitarians on some points of biblical interpretation, just as they would disagree with me. In my own journey with the biblical truth, I've not been concerned with fitting into a particular camp or assenting to every item on a checklist that marks one as theologically kosher. In fact, my own position is either almost-complementarian or nearly-egalitarian, depending how you look at it.

Yet I have changed my view on women and ministry, and some of my friends have shaken their head in disappointment, thinking that I have sold out to the cultural tide of feminism by adopting a fashionably left-leaning version of evangelicalism. My own perspective is that I have simply followed the testimony of biblical texts that affirm women can and should be involved in pastoral care and the church's teaching ministry. Let me tell you about my journey.

During my late teenage years, my views on women were largely shaped by military culture. I joined the Army at age seventeen and adopted the maxim of German philosopher Friedrich Nietzsche: "Man shall be trained for war, and woman for the recreation of the warrior: all else is folly." Women were mainly sexual playthings—though finding a *bourgeois babe* willing to satisfy my unbridled lusts was not particularly easy. Fortunately my conversion to Christ at age twenty led to change in a great many areas of my life, including my view of women and relationships. But in my early theological education I took to a patriarchal view very naturally. I was greatly influenced by complementarians such as John Piper, John MacArthur, and Wayne Grudem—men I still admire and respect even if I must now depart company from them on this issue.

As an undergraduate ministry student, I did not hesitate to voice my complementarian views during discussions among fellow students, friends, family members, and teachers. I will never forget the time an equally devout egalitarian woman called me a "patriarchal, androcentric, chauvinistic misogynist." At the time I did not know what all those fancy words meant, but the saliva foaming at her mouth led me to think she was calling me something very, very bad. I also attended a conservative evangelical church that was strongly complementarian, to the point that it even forbade women ushers. Over the course of time, however, four significant events led me to doubt the complementarian position and, finally, to abandon it altogether.

First, I began to question why we never had female worship leaders in our Sunday worship services. After all, "worship leader" is not even a biblical office. Ephesians 4:11–12 does not say that God gave some to be "apostles, prophets, teaching-shepherds, and worship leaders." Moreover, I would hardly call worship leader a teaching ministry. I didn't understand the restriction, but I went along with it just to make extra sure that feminists didn't get a foothold in our church. At the same time, my church stopped allowing women to lead worship at midweek Bible studies—I'm talking about a woman with a guitar picking three choruses for a group of eight people to sing in someone's living room. I approached one of the pastors and was told the reason for the prohibition was that a worship leader *leads* worshipers into the presence of God; therefore, it needed to be a male role. But as I thought about it later, I remembered that a theme in Hebrews is how Jesus leads us all into the presence of God (see Heb. 4:16; 10:19, 35). What is more, surely the doctrine of the priesthood of all believers should preclude us from seeing anyone other than Jesus Christ as a mediator of access to God! My dear pastor had not convinced me, and doubts began to encroach upon my mind.

Second, my confidence in the biblical integrity of the complementarian ship was shaken simply by reading carefully Acts and the Pauline letters, in which it was evident that Paul had a lot of female coworkers. I got the impression they did more than teach other women, instruct children, and manage the flower arrangements. This sense was reinforced when I attended a Ben Witherington lecture on Romans 16 at Morling College, which not only confirmed my suspicions about Paul's female coworkers, but also challenged many of my complementarian assumptions.[5]

Third, I finally said goodbye to complementarianism after hearing about what happened at the *Together For the Gospel* conference (T4G) in 2006. Initially this fantastic conference was open to both men and women, but after it began to fill up, the organizers stopped accepting applications from women. They even asked women to give up their places so that more men could attend. Given that this was a conference geared toward pastors, if only men can be pastors, those actions seemed to make sense. But—and this is what irked me—the organizers of T4G did not request that *all* nonpastors give up their spots. No, they requested only that women give up their places and prohibited them from attending. Any man who had an interest in the conference could attend, whether or not he was involved in pastoral ministry.

This created a situation in which some pew-sitting couch potato who had no ministry ambitions but wanted to hear some good teaching could go to T4G because he was male, but a woman who was actually involved in university ministry, foreign missions, or parish work could not go. I blogged on this and got quite a response. Some said, "Well, you weren't at T4G; what do you know?" But I also got responses from people who were there, agreed with what I said, but were afraid to speak up lest they be accused of being egalitarian. I got the feeling that, in some circles, in order to be a complementarian-approved dude, you had to be willing not only to salute at the complementarian flagpole but also to impale your mother, wife, sister, or daughter on it every once in a while to demonstrate your loyalty. It was at this point that I ceased to identify myself as complementarian.[6]

Fourth, I knew I had to sort out this issue in my mind once and for all, so I reached for the jugular and began an intense and rigorous study of 1 Timothy 2:11–14. This passage is at the epicenter of the debate about women and ministry. Previously, I had maintained that Paul's argument in the passage is not culturally situated but rooted in the creation story of Genesis 1–3. The explanatory clause explaining Paul's prohibition about women teaching men— "for [*gar*] Adam was formed first"—showed that Paul's rationale was lodged in the order of creation rather than any circumstance specific to Ephesus.

The problem I faced was that Paul's argument in 1 Corinthians 11:2–16 about women covering their heads was obviously related to Greco-Roman culture, yet Paul still employed the same kind of theological argument from creation. I could not bring myself to believe that Paul meant to provide us with a universal and prescriptive theology of hats and headwear. The prohibition against women prophesying with heads uncovered was anchored in the cultural setting of Corinth; it touched on issues of female propriety in the Greco-Roman world. Thus, by analogy, the allusions to Genesis 1–3 in 1 Timothy 2:11–14 did not *demand* that the prohibition against women teaching men be universal rather than cultural.[7] Yes, Eve was deceived. Paul makes much of that point in 1 Timothy 2:14 in relation to women in Ephesus being gullible. But in 2 Corinthians 11:3 he warns that any of the Corinthians, male or female, could be deceived in a similar way: "But I am afraid that as the serpent deceived Eve by its cunning, your thoughts will be led astray from a sincere and pure devotion to Christ" [NRSV].

Both men and women can fall into the complacency and deception of Eve.

Additionally, women did teach and prophesy elsewhere in the New Testament. I had to ask, how did the prohibition in 1 Timothy 2:11–14 relate to the rest of the New Testament? I realized that only one of two conclusions sufficed. Either a post-Pauline disciple who did not share Paul's convictions about women wrote 1 Timothy, or the prohibition against women teaching men in 1 Timothy 2:11–14 was primarily related to cultural circumstances transpiring in Ephesus, to which Paul was responding. This does not make Paul's prohibition purely relative or irrelevant to our time. But I think it does mean that we have to do some serious wrestling with the social context of 1 Timothy 2:11–14 in our exegesis and with our own cultural context in application. After reading various commentaries, I came to the conclusion that women can teach, preach, and lead in the local church. I confess to remaining a bit uncertain on whether women should occupy the highest leadership positions in the church, based on lingering exegetical and ecumenical concerns. But women teachers and women pastors—you preach it, girl!

So that's my journey. What I want to do in this book is not push my view down anyone's throat, but rather share my trek through Scripture and identify the issues one has to sort through to come to a conclusion on this topic. Such a study must deal principally with Paul, as Paul's letters contain the majority of the disputed texts on women and leadership. Indeed, there is no area of Pauline studies that I find more confusing, more emotive, and more heated than the subject of Paul on women. I confess that I have changed my mind on certain points several times. Some of the most volatile debates I have participated in have been on this subject. I have been called both a "liberal" and a "fundamentalist" for views I have expounded on Paul and women. As such, this book will contain a mixture of exegesis of Paul's letters and a narration of my own journey through the subject.

Chapter 1

Who's Who in the Zoo?

So far I've used some terms like "complementarian" and "egalitarian," "patriarchal hierarchialist" and "feminist." If you aren't already familiar with these views, then here is a summary. Generally speaking, complementarians advocate that God made human beings equal in worth but distinct in role, with leadership roles assigned to men so that women cannot lead or have authority over men. The complementarian position is represented by, among others, the Council for Biblical Manhood and Womanhood. Generally speaking, egalitarians believe that men and women are equal in both value and role, so that women may occupy any position of ministry leadership open to men. The egalitarian position is represented by Christians for Biblical Equality. The two groups exchange views about Paul and women, women in ministry, gender roles in marriage, and women in the public square through various publications.[8]

However, in reality there are more than two positions on this topic, as evidenced by the chart on the following page.[9]

- On the extreme left (no pun intended) are Christian feminists, who want to liberate women from oppression and free them from the shackles of a male-dominated society. This goal often involves reading against the grain of biblical texts, since they are allegedly written from a masculine and patriarchal viewpoint.
- What sets evangelical egalitarians apart from Christian feminists is their commitment to biblical authority and their unwillingness to read the Bible through the grid of

Egalitarian Position				Complementarian Position		
Christian Feminist	Boundary	Evangelical Egalitarian	Boundary	Moderate Compl.	Boundary	Hierarchical Compl.
Women are an oppressed minority who need to experience their own exodus or liberation from bondage and be freed from male domination. Women must be promoted at every opportunity.	Biblical authority	Men and women are equals in ministry and women can hold any office in the church. Ministry is based on giftedness and qualification and not gender.	Women elders	Women are encouraged to engage in any ministry role besides that of elder, teaching elder, or senior pastor. Women can preach under the oversight of a male pastor and can occupy teaching positions in a seminary or parachurch organization.	Women teaching men	Women can have important leadership roles in ministries to other women and children, but they are expressly prohibited from any office or function where they would be exercising authority over men, especially teaching and preaching in a church or seminary.

feminist liberation. Evangelical egalitarians believe that the gospel includes an inherent equality principle, that spiritual gifts do not come in pink or blue, and that scriptural prohibitions against women teaching or having authority over men are specific and local rather than universal.

- What separates moderate complementarians from evangelical egalitarians is the belief that women are restricted from church offices such as bishop, senior pastor, or teaching elder. However, moderate complementarians permit women to teach men under certain conditions within the church and in positions outside the local church (such as seminaries).

- What separates hierarchical complementarians from moderate complementarians is that the former prohibit women from teaching any men within the local church. At the same time, hierarchical complementarians promote women's leadership in women's and children's ministries.

The reason I have included this chart is that it shows that the debate is not completely cut and dried, with the bad guys in black hats on the left and the good guys in white hats on the right. Within evangelicalism there is a spectrum of opinion and practice on this subject. Many criticisms of Christian feminists cannot simply be pasted onto evangelical egalitarians, and many criticisms of evangelical egalitarians could also be leveled against moderate complementarians.

Evangelicals participating in this debate always appeals to the apostle Paul to substantiate their position. But therein lies the problem, since Paul cannot simultaneously be both an advocate and an opponent of women preachers and female ordination. We need to ask in all honesty and with integrity, "What did Paul really say about women?" To study this question takes a great deal of discipline and requires listening to the text of Scripture even when we feel uncomfortable about what it says. We also need to engage graciously a variety of believers' opinions; acknowledge our own biases, both cultural and denominational; and seek to understand the context of Paul's world. What I want to do in this ebook is provide some insight into the historical and cultural status of women in the ancient world, survey the pertinent texts of Paul's letters, and, finally, provide a recipe for working and worshiping with believers who take a different stance on this issue. But before we go down that path, I want to make you think a bit first!

Chapter 2

Fretting Over Phoebe

Allow me to show you how a close reading of the biblical text can cause a meltdown in long-held assumptions about women and ministry.

I love messing with my students. It can be done a number of ways. Taking some of their most basic and unguarded assumptions and exploding them is nearly as fun as putting a bottle rocket under Grandpa's rocking chair when he's napping. Leading them down obscure exegetical caves and trekking through hidden historical ravines is equally rewarding, as I get to see students experience the awe and thrill of new discoveries. Theological education should be about testing long-held assumptions and discovering new possibilities in theology and practice. One place I routinely do that with students is the topic of Paul and women. Let me give you an example. During my Romans class, at some point in the term, I ask the students four questions about Paul's letter to the Roman churches:

1. ***So who actually wrote Romans?***

   "Paul," they immediately reply in chorus.

   "No," I retort, "Who physically sat down and penned the letter to Paul's dictation?"

   Blank faces, deep thoughts, then some bright spark will blurt out, "Oh, oh, that guy, what's his name, um, Tertius."

   "Correct-a-mundo" comes the teacher's approving reply, pointing to Romans 16:22, "I, Tertius, who wrote down this letter, greet you in the Lord."

   Moving on, we come to the next big question!

2. *So who delivered the letter to the Romans? Who was Paul's envoy?*

Confused faces, odd looks. How can they be expected to know that?

"Turn with me to Romans 16," I say, and together we read the following: "I commend to you our sister Phoebe, a deacon of the church in Cenchreae. I ask you to receive her in the Lord in a way worthy of his people and to give her any help she may need from you, for she has been the benefactor of many people, including me" (Rom. 16:1–2, emphasis added).

Then we have a cool discussion about the meaning of "deacon" and "benefactor" and the role of letter carriers in antiquity. It gives a good starting point to talk about Christian ministry and patron-client relationships in the context of the Greco-Roman world.

"So then, if Phoebe is a deacon, Paul's benefactor, and if he trusted her to take this important letter to the Romans, then Phoebe must have been a woman of great abilities and good character in Paul's mind. Do you agree?"

Heads nod in agreement.

3. *Okay, and if the Romans had any questions about the letter, such as: like "What is the righteousness of God?" or "Who is this wretched man that Paul refers to about halfway through?"then who do you think would be the first person that they would ask?*

Eyes wide opened, some mouths gaping, others looking a bit irritated.

Then I provocatively add: "Could it be that the first person to publicly read and teach about Romans was a woman? If so, what does that tell you about women and teaching roles in the early church?"

The end result is an "Aha" moment for some students, and a mix of confusion and frustration for others.

4. *(Then comes the big question.) Think about it, people. This is Romans—Paul's attempt to prevent a potentially fractious cluster of house churches in Rome from dividing over debates about the Jewish law. This is Paul's effort to return to Jerusalem with all of the Gentile churches behind him. This is Paul's one chance to garner support from the Roman churches for a mission to Spain. This is Romans, his greatest letter-essay, the most influential letter in the history of Western thought, and the singularly greatest piece of Christian theology. Now if Paul was so opposed to women teaching men anytime and anywhere, why on earth would he send a woman like Phoebe to deliver this vitally important letter* and *to be his personal representative in Rome? Why not Timothy, Titus, or any other dude? Why Phoebe?*

Some students nod in agreement, others flick over to 1 Timothy 2:12, others sit back and just think about it.

I'm careful to stress that this observation from Romans is not the be-all and end-all of debates about women in ministry. There are other texts, contexts, and interpretations that we must deal with. But I point out that, taken at face value, Paul seemed to have no problem with women having some kind of speaking role in the churches. If he did have qualms, then sending Phoebe to Rome was a really, really odd thing to do. My conclusion is that Paul's commendation of Deacon Phoebe, her position as his benefactor, and her role as both a letter carrier and his representative to the Roman churches indicates that women were part of the didactic life of the church, and Paul specifically encouraged it. That is the central thesis of this little ebook! While there may be male headship in marriage and even restrictions on some forms of ministry for women, nonetheless it is clear to me that a cursory reading of Paul's letters shows that women participated in the teaching ministry of the early church.

Chapter 3
Women in the Pauline Churches

Paul says a lot of things about women in passing, but sometimes his instructions for the churches focus on issues of gender, culture, and Christian identity. To these passages we now turn.

Heads, Hair, and Hats (1 Corinthians 11:2–16)

[2]I praise you for remembering me in everything and for holding to the traditions just as I passed them on to you. [3]But I want you to realize that the head of every man is Christ, and the head of the woman is man,and the head of Christ is God. [4]Every man who prays or prophesies with his head covered dishonors his head. [5]But every woman who prays or prophesies with her head uncovered dishonors her head—it is the same as having her head shaved. [6]For if a woman does not cover her head, she might as well have her hair cut off; but if it is a disgrace for a woman to have her hair cut off or her head shaved, then she should cover her head. [7]A man ought not to cover his head,since he is the image and glory of God; but woman is the glory of man. [8]For man did not come from woman, but woman from man; [9]neither was man created for woman, but woman for man. [10]It is for this reason that a woman ought to have authority over her own1 head, because of the angels. [11]Nevertheless, in the Lord woman is not independent of man, nor is man independent of woman. [12]For as woman came from man, so also man is born of woman. But everything comes from God.

[13]Judge for yourselves: Is it proper for a woman to pray to God with her head uncovered? [14]Does not the very nature of things teach you that if a man has long hair, it is a disgrace to

him, [15]but that if a woman has long hair, it is her glory? For long hair is given to her as a covering. [16]If anyone wants to be contentious about this, we have no other practice—nor do the churches of God.

Paul's instructions about the appropriate attire for men and women in corporate worship is connected to issues of authority, gender, creation, culture, and the glory of God. It is a complex text to get into and one that baffles young Christians and seasoned scholars alike. Whenever I read this passage, I'm reminded of two things. First, in the movie *My Big Fat Greek Wedding* (2002), there is a scene where Maria Portokalos tells her daughter Toula, "Let me tell you something, Toula. The man is the head, but the woman is the neck. And she can turn the head any way she wants." Yes, that's funny, but it does make male headship something that is acceptable to women only for the purpose of manipulating it for their own peculiar ends.

Second, a former female student of mine, now a minister in the Church of Scotland, recounts how in her early teens she forgot to bring her hat to church. One of the elders of the church would not let her in the hall with an uncovered head and told her to go and look for a hat in the cloak room. When she pleaded that she still could not find one, the elder begrudgingly permitted her to enter the hall, but muttered in disgust, "Go on in there then, you harlot." The young girl went home and asked her mother, "What's a harlot?" Not a nice thing to call a thirteen-year-old girl because she doesn't have a hat on! Strange as it is to us, Paul is concerned that the Corinthians have an appropriate view of heads, hair, and hats.

Paul affirms on several occasions the headship of the husband over the wife. He is the authority of the household and exercises loving care in his relations with his family (1 Cor. 11:3; Eph. 5:22–33; Col. 3:18). In the passage quoted above, Paul states: "But I want you to realize that the head of every man is Christ, and the head of every woman is man, and the head of Christ is God" (1 Cor. 11:3). The meaning of the word *kephalē* as it appears here depends on whether we understand it as "head" in the sense of authority or "head" as meaning a source (like the head of a river). Is Paul merely saying that the husband is the "source" of the wife or is he the "authority" over the wife? The fact is that Paul can use *kephalē* as either "source" (e.g., Eph. 4:15–16) or "authority" (e.g. Eph. 1:22), depending on the context. In line with a spate of recent commentaries, I am convinced that here *kephalē* in 1 Corinthians 11:3 means "head" with connotations of "authority," "pre-eminence," and "honor."[10] Paul relates headship to what men and women do with their actual heads during corporate worship. His concern is that honor and glory accrue to God by the devotion and decorum of Christian worship as demonstrated in, of all things, head dress.

Importantly, Paul is not arguing here for a chain of command along the lines of God → Christ → Man → Woman. Note the order of the couplets as they appear: Christ/Man, then Husband/Wife, and finally God/Christ, which does not lend itself to a hierarchy from the Father at the top with women at the bottom.[11] Paul's argument draws an analogy to the effect that both *men and women* should not dishonor their respective heads. Paul intends to correct male behavior just as much as female behavior. Indeed, headship is something that binds men and women together under Christ![12] There is indeed a hierarchy of relations between the persons mentioned in the various couplets, but one that must also be understood in light of the gospel, where Paul affirms mutuality, reciprocity, and the value of others in the relationships that characterize the new creation.[13] Thus, the husband is no dictator or despot, but he leads and loves his wife as Christ leads and loves the church, that is, in a self-sacrificing way (Eph. 5:25).

The concept of male headship, which I think indisputable (based on what Paul says), has often been used as a mantra for limiting the ministries that women are allowed to engage in. The irony is that in 1 Corinthians 11:2–16 Paul seems to be stating the exact opposite, namely, that as long as creational gender distinctions are maintained and as long as women dress with modesty and decorum, then men and women are both free to engage in the same activities of prayer and prophecy in corporate worship. Family headship is determined by gender, but church ministry is determined by divine calling and spiritual gifts.

The issue of head-coverings in 1 Corinthians 11:2–16 strikes readers as rather foreign, and it is a difficult passage for interpreters to engage with. This passage is a good example of the cultural distance between our world and the world that Paul inhabited in places like Roman Corinth. So some background information will illuminate the text for us. First, we need to take into account that Christian meetings took place in semipublic places. Whether that was in a lecture hall, down by a river, in a small shop, or even in someone's house (such as in an atrium), these sorts of places were often visible to outsiders. So Paul would naturally be concerned with what transpired in the Corinthian's corporate worship because what they were doing would probably be visible to their neighbors, friends, and any passersby.

Second, the emphasis on veils and head-coverings is because a woman's hair was considered to be sexually alluring, and women were not to dress in provocative ways to suggest that they were sexually available. In Roman society a well-covered woman was making a statement of her respectability and that she was not to be leered at or propositioned. Paul does not make any injunctions about women's attire outside of corporate worship, but he does provide instructions about women wearing veils in worship when they are drawing attention to themselves in prayer or prophecy. It is her veil in fact that authorizes her to speak before the assembly. Paul doesn't want men to cover their heads perhaps because it was too reminiscent of what men wore during pagan sacrifices, or else it was to reinforce the gender differentiation from women in worship. By not covering or covering their heads, men and women both reflect the glory of God as God made them.

Third, long hair on a man was often a mark of homosexuality, so it was to be avoided (though what they considered "long" might not be what we consider long—like Willie Nelson long). Paul considers long hair on a woman to be a type of extra veil that nature has provided to protect women from the shame of a shaven head (and a shaven head was a sign of humiliation). The hair of speakers in church was to bolster the distinctiveness of male and female.

Moving from background to the passage itself, Brian Rosner and Roy Ciampa point out that Paul affirms three things here: (1) respect for a creation mandate to maintain and celebrate gender distinctions between the sexes; (2) a respect for culturally specific ways of guarding moral and sexual purity; and (3) a commitment to fully integrating women and their gifts into the experience of the worshiping community.[14] All in all, Paul is focusing on humanity as created by God, as male and female, and on living out the specific calling of their God-given gender in a way appropriate to the cultural environs of ancient Corinth, so that God is truly glorified by their corporate worship of praise, prayer, and prophecy.

Paul's remarks are principally concerned with behavior in the Corinthian's worship that might be perceived as a denial of the differentiation between men and women according to culturally extant notions of gender identity. Accordingly, women were not to be masculine, nor were men to be effeminate in their dress and bearing while speaking to the assembly, before God, and perhaps even in the presence of angels. Women were also not to dress in a way that could give the impression that they were sexually available. By denying God-intended gender identities and dressing in ways that could be deemed risqué, the Corinthians were potentially bringing shame on themselves in the view of outsiders. Paul affirms the equality of their roles in corporate worship while he instructs them on the proper attire for such worship to take place.[15]

Women and Silence (1 Corinthians 14:33–36)

God isn't a God of disorder but of peace. Like in all the churches of God's people, [34]the women should be quiet during the meeting. They are not allowed to talk. Instead, they need to get under control, just as the Law says. [35]If they want to learn something, they should ask their husbands at home. It is disgraceful for a woman to talk during the meeting.

[36]Did the word of God originate with you? Has it come only to you? (Common English Bible)

In 1 Corinthians 14, Paul provides instructions about the regulation of public worship especially in relation to the display of spiritual gifts. After insisting on orderliness in the exercise of tongues and the uttering of prophecies (1 Cor. 14:26–33a), in our received text of the letter, Paul next enjoins them to orderliness by commanding women to remain silent in corporate worship (1 Cor. 14:33b–35). For some this text is a manifesto for putting women in their place; for others it is a piece of deplorable misogyny.

Some have even argued that verses 34–35 are an interpolation inserted here by some sexist scribe who wanted to use Paul as leverage against outspoken women (note how the NRSV places verses 33b–35 in parentheses!). There are two reasons for this. (1) There is curious textual evidence that verses 34–35 were considered spurious by some copyists and were moved around to find a better place for it. A handful of manuscripts place 14:34–35 *after* 14:40 so that the passage jumps from 14:33 to 14:36. These include three bilingual Greek-Latin manuscripts, two Old Latin texts, a single Vulgate text, and two Latin Fathers; and a few manuscripts have marginal notes indicating that some scribes saw a possible textual corruption in these verses.

(2) There is alleged to be internal evidence that 1 Corinthians 14:34–35 is an interpolation since the injunction for women to be silent purportedly contradicts 11:5, 13, where women could prophesy and pray in public worship. In addition, one can read 14:33a and then jump to 14:36 and it does make sense. The problem with the interpolation theory is, however, that it rests on rather slim evidence. The fact is that every extant manuscript of 1 Corinthians contains 14:33b–35, even if a few cheeky scribes thought that they could move it to a more appropriate place in the same paragraph. Furthermore, if a scribe had interpolated verses 33a–35 in order to force women to be silent, one must wonder why the same scribe did not omit portions of 11:2–16 about women praying and prophesying in church.[16]

The most likely explanation for 1 Corinthians 14:33b–35 is that Paul is concerned with how wives related to and interacted with their husbands during public worship. Note how 14:33a and 14:40 focus on order and propriety in assembled meetings. Paul is not issuing a broad blanket prohibition of women speaking at all in church because 11.2–16 and a pancake stack of other texts refer instead to women speaking in church. It is the *type* of speaking and not the *possibility* of wives speaking that Paul prohibits. Most likely, Paul envisages wives doing something like interrupting a speaker to ask their husbands questions during prophecies or tongues, or else speaking over someone in order to be heard. Perhaps women were even questioning or contradicting their husbands before the church in matters concerning prophecy or scriptural interpretation. If women are genuinely interested in learning and discussion, that is more than fine, but the home is the proper place for that rather than being interruptive or contentious.

Paul also states here that he wants the Corinthians to follow the law (1 Cor. 14:34b, probably the patriarchal narratives that are filled with examples of women who are respectful of their husbands), and he offers the example of the Palestinian churches (who probably had a stricter view of women's roles than Greek or Roman cultures) in order to ensure decorum in corporate worship and to encourage wives to respect their husbands. This safeguards believers from marital divisions and prevents the church's inclusion of women in worship from being mistaken for one of the secret and orgiastic mystery cults that had reputations for feminine excesses.[17]

Mutual Submission?

[21]Submit to one another out of reverence for Christ. [22]Wives, submit yourselves to your own husbands as you do to the Lord. [23]For the husband is the head of the wife as Christ is the head of the church, his body, of which he is the Savior. [24]Now as the church submits to Christ, so also wives should submit to their husbands in everything. (Eph. 5:21–24).

[4]The wife does not have authority over her own body but yields it to her husband. In the same way, the husband does not have authority over his own body but yields it to his wife. (1 Cor. 7:4).

[8]For man did not come from woman, but woman from man; [9]neither was man created for woman, but woman for man. [10]It is for this reason that a woman ought to have authority over her own head, because of the angels. [11]Nevertheless, in the Lord woman is not independent of man, nor is man independent of woman. [12]For as woman came from man, so also man is born of woman. But everything comes from God. (1 Cor. 11:8–12).

¹⁵You know that the household of Stephanas were the first converts in Achaia, and they have devoted themselves to the service of the Lord's people. I urge you, brothers and sisters, ¹⁶to submit to such people and to everyone who joins in the work and labors at it. (1 Cor. 16:15–16).

In Paul's instructions on relationships within the household, he provides a general template for the relations between husbands and wives, masters and slaves, and parents and children that follows general custom albeit infused with Christian virtues (Eph. 5:21–6.9; Col. 3:18–4.1; Titus 2:1–10). There is no question that Paul indeed refers to wives submitting to husbands (Eph. 5:22; Col. 3:18; Titus 2:5). But it is curious to many people that Paul's household code in Ephesians 5:22–33 is prefaced with a mention of corporate submission in 5:21: "Submit to one another out of reverence for Christ." Does this moderate or water down Paul's instructions about wives submitting to husbands by implying that, on some occasions at least, husbands should submit to their wives?

Well, "moderate" and "water down" are the wrong ways to put it. Still, Ephesians 5:22–24 should be taken in light of 5:21, and 5:21 plainly states that every person can find themselves subject to another person. Paul doesn't say "every person" should submit to "every person" in some kind of anti-hierarchical anarchy. More likely, the church of God exists in a network of relationships where submission to other persons in some office or task is necessary. When such submission happens, one is following the example of Christ, who submitted himself to God the Father.

Now then, should husbands ever submit to their wives? Is there any mutual submission in marriage at all? Although some chaps like Wayne Grudem cannot imagine Paul ever telling husbands to submit to their wives, Paul says as clear as Aspen air that wives and husbands do not have authority over their own bodies but yield them up to the authority of their wife or husband (see 1 Cor. 7:4). Sounds a lot like mutual submission to me! That coheres perfectly with what we find elsewhere, where Paul says that in the Lord there is *interdependence* between husbands and wives (1 Cor. 11:11). I think male headship is in a sense normative, but headship will mean bowing that head to the wife in many matters pertaining to marriage, so "mutual submission" is in fact an accurate term.

What about at church? Could men ever submit to wives there? I think we can reasonably infer that this did happen at Corinth. In Corinth we read of two major households, those of Stephanas (male) and Chloe (female). Both sent delegations to Paul either giving reports of bad behavior (1 Cor. 1:11; 11:18) or sending Paul a list of questions that needed answering (7:1). My premise is that often church leadership and household leadership went hand in hand, all the more probably since Paul never mentions elders in the Corinthian letters, so the de facto church leaders were the recognized household heads. In order to bring some semblance of order to the mayhem in Corinth, Paul tells the Corinthians to submit to Stephanus's house and to "everyone who joins in the work and labors at it" (16:15–16).

I think that later phrase about submitting to Christian laborers included women; here are a few reasons why. (1) The other major household in Corinth we know about was headed by a women, Chloe, and she may have been similarly active like Stephanas. Chloe is perhaps one of "such people" who should be submitted to as a house leader/church leader in Corinth. Paul specifically mentions Stephanas only because he was there in Ephesus while Paul was writing the letter and perhaps even delivered the letter to the Corinthians (though admittedly I'm inferring this). (2) Chloe could arguably be somewhat like Phoebe in Cenchreae (which was near Corinth), a wealthy women involved in church ministry or else actively supporting the ministry financially. (3) Paul refers to the "work" of women in ministry elsewhere (Rom. 16:6, 12; Phil. 4:3). So if one submits to "workers" and if women like Phoebe and Chloe were such "workers" in service to the Lord's holy people in the Corinthian area, it stands to reason that Paul would expect people to submit to their ministries![18]

Paul's Cohort of Female Coworkers

Paul's letters make many references to women and their ministry roles in the churches with which he was associated. There are clear indications that some women even had a prominent part in the teaching ministry and worship life of the early churches. Two prominent coworkers of Paul were Priscilla and Aquila (Acts 18:2; Rom. 16:3; 1 Cor. 16:19; 2 Tim. 4:19), and Luke tells us that both Priscilla and Aquila took Apollos aside and "explained to him the way of God more accurately" (Acts 18:26). The word *exethento* ("explained") is in the third person plural and implies that both Priscilla and Aquila did the explaining, not just Aquila. Paul writes in the letter to Titus that older women were to instruct younger women (Titus 2:3–4).

Paul refers to the gift of prophecy on several occasions (Rom. 12:6; 1 Cor. 12:10, 28; 13:2; 14:1; Eph. 4:11). The prophetic office was evidently widespread in the early church, and it kept the living voice of Jesus fresh in the early Christian movement. On the day of Pentecost, Peter explained the momentous event of the outpouring of the Holy Spirit with its accompanying phenomena by citing Joel 2:28–29, that in the final days God will pour his Spirit on all people, and men and women will prophesy (Acts 2:17–18). We also know that there were female prophets who prophesied in Christian gatherings that included men (Acts 21:9; 1 Cor. 11:5). Note also that the offices of prophet and teacher are explicitly linked in Acts 13:1. If prophecy is didactic (i.e., not just foretelling but a forth-telling of God's word) and authoritative (i.e., an inspired word that comes from God), the conclusion we must reach is that women did indeed teach men with an authoritative prophetic word.

Several women such as Priscilla, Euodia, and Syntyche are called Paul's "coworkers" (*synergos*) in the ministry of the gospel (Rom. 16:3; Phil. 4:3), and the same word group is used elsewhere to describe the ministry of prominent male Christian leaders in the Pauline circle (Rom. 16:9, 21; 1 Cor. 16:15–16; 2 Cor. 8:23; Phil. 2:25; Col. 4:11; 1 Thess. 3:2; Philem. 1, 24). The type of ministry that these women discharged is not explicitly stated, but it was clearly alongside Paul, and we have no immediate reason for thinking that their activities were radically different from what Timothy, Titus, Justus, Luke, Mark, Demas, Aristarchus, or Epaphroditus did. Most likely these women worked beside Paul as part of his evangelistic and church planting activities. In Paul's various lists of spiritual gifts and offices he never associates a gift or office with a certain gender (Rom. 12:4–8; 1 Cor. 12:4–6, 28–31; Eph. 4:11–12). The ministries of the church are based on divine calling and spiritual charisma, not on gender. This comports with the giving of the Spirit in Peter's speech on Pentecost, where it is reported twice that God pours out his Spirit on men and women alike (Acts 2:17–21).

More generally we find Paul saying that Christians are to teach each other with no reference to gender roles or limitations (Rom. 15:14; Col. 3:16). In Corinth, where Paul was not shy about gender issues, he states: "When you come together, each of you has a hymn, or a word of instruction, a revelation, a tongue or an interpretation" with no addendum on who may instruct (1 Cor. 14:26). No gender restriction on that score either.

At the end of Romans we find a reference to Phoebe, to whom Paul entrusted the deliverance of his letter to Rome. She is called a "servant [*diakonos*] of the church in Cenchreae" (Rom. 16:1). She may have served the church to which she belonged or held an office equivalent to that of deacon. Either is possible; nothing is said of how she served. One must wonder why Paul chose this woman to be the envoy for this important letter. Part of the reason was undoubtedly that she was Paul's "patron" or "benefactor" (*prostatis*) and was probably a woman of some means or status. Paul also commends her in the formal sense of introducing her to the house churches in Rome. If she was literate, she presumably even read the letter aloud to the house churches and, who knows, perhaps she even fielded questions about its contents since she was an official delegate of Paul. This is admittedly speculative, but it is eminently plausible, given the setting. In the same section Paul mentions Mary, Tryphena, Tryphosa, and Persis who "work hard in the Lord"—an expression that likely denotes ministry in the gospel (Rom. 16:6, 12).

In Romans 16 there is also the mention of a female apostle: "Greet Andronicus and Junia, my fellow Jews who have been in prison with me. They are *outstanding among the apostles*, and they were in Christ before I was" (Rom. 16:7, emphasis added). Two points of interpretation are contested here. (1) The Greek name *Iounian* can be masculine (Junias) or feminine (Junia), depending on how one accents the original Greek text. (2) Does the expression *episēmoi en tois apostolois* mean "outstanding among the apostles" (NIV) or "well known to the apostles" (ESV)?

To answer these questions we can begin by noting that the feminine name "Junia" was accepted almost unanimously by early commentators, and there is wide attestation for women named Junia from ancient inscriptions and other Greek literature (250 instances, in fact), but there are no known references to the masculine Junias. Similarly, the case for an exclusive translation of "well known to the apostles" hangs on a thin thread of evidence and was not the view of early commentators, who regarded Junia as an apostle. For example, John Chrysostom wrote: "O how great is the devotion of this woman that she should be counted worthy of the appellation of apostle!" (*Homily on Romans*, 31.2). The attempts to reassign her gender or to exclude her from the apostles springs from an uneasiness about the natural interpretation of the text, namely, that Junia was a women who was outstanding among the apostles—an interpretation that caused no discomfort or anxiety to Christians in the early centuries of the church.

It is possible that Andronicus and Junia, perhaps a married couple, were apostles in the sense of one who is sent out by a church like a missionary, such as Epaphroditus in Philippians 2:25 and Titus in 2 Corinthians 8:23. However, such people are usually designated by the church that they have come from as (lit.) "apostles of the churches" or "your apostle" or even like Phoebe as a "servant [deacon] of the church of Cenchreae."[19] Alternatively, Andronicus and Junia may have been apostles in the sense of being witnesses to Jesus' resurrection and were commissioned at that time for the ministry that they were now undertaking outside of Palestine (1 Cor. 15:6–7). That is supported by the fact that Paul says that they were "in Christ before I was," so that they were probably converted in Palestine some time around AD 30–32. The only other appearances of the word "apostle" in Romans describe Paul's commission to go to the Gentiles (Rom. 1:1; 11:13). Eldon Epp has recently concluded: "It remains a fact that there was a woman apostle, explicitly so named, in the earliest generation of Christianity, and contemporary Christians—laypeople and clergy—must (and eventually will) face up to it."[20]

In the early church there were women who were the heads of households, and they likely exercised some form of leadership in house churches that came under the aegis of their benefaction (Acts 16:14–15; 17:4; 1 Cor. 1:11; Col. 4:15). For example, Stephanas was the head of a household in the city of Corinth and a prominent leader in the church there (1 Cor. 1:16; 16:15–17). Should we say the same of women like Nympha concerning "the church [that meets] in her house" (Col. 4:15) in Laodicea? Or of Chloe in relation to her household also in Corinth (1 Cor. 1:11)? Women like Nympha and Chloe may have acted as leaders in some sense although we have no explicit evidence from the first century to indicate how or in what precise capacity.

The Egalitarian Manifesto (Galatians 3:26–29)

Was Paul a full-fledged egalitarian? Well, according to many, at the end of Galatians 3, Paul produced a virtual manifesto of Christian equality:

> [26]So in Christ Jesus you are all children of God through faith, [27]for all of you who were baptized into Christ have clothed yourselves with Christ. [28]There is neither Jew nor Gentile, neither slave nor free, nor is there male and female, for you are all one in Christ Jesus. [29]If you belong to Christ, then you are Abraham's seed, and heirs according to the promise.

In the midst of his argument in Galatians that Gentiles do not have to undergo circumcision in order to be heirs of Abraham, Paul writes: "There is neither Jew nor Gentile, neither slave nor free, nor is there *male and female*, for you are all one in Christ Jesus" (Gal. 3:28, emphasis added). Obviously a lot rides on what Paul means here. Now Paul is not suggesting that for Christians gender ceases to exist, as if God only looks at people from the neck up, thus obliterating the physical distinction between men and women. Rebirth does not mean that we are ever after unisex and can use the same washrooms at church. Nor is Paul stating that this teaching only applies to salvation or spiritual things. What Paul is saying is that the new creation means the obliteration of the distinctions that have separated human beings from one another in the past.

The primary dialogue partner here is not feminists or hierarchicalists, but Jewish Christians who want to retain the privileges of their ethnic identity. For Paul, neither race, nor class, nor gender places one closer to the throne of God. God intended to create one family, not two or more families, and Abraham's family has children from every nation, rich and poor, male and female. This underscores the equality principle of the gospel, where no one can boast that they have the inside track to God or can insinuate that they are better or more useful than any other person. While the primary content of Galatians 3:27–28 focuses on soteriology (salvation), we must keep in mind that it is also related to ecclesiology (church) and pneumatology (the Holy Spirit). The point here is not merely equality before God, but unity within the church created by the bonds of baptism and ratified by the gift of the Holy Spirit.

Paul's statement is a powerful and poignant reminder of Christian togetherness amidst manifold diversity. What is more, the power of the new creation at work in Christians through the Spirit abolishes the use of gender, class, and ethnicity as a means to power and status. Such elements now exist only in subordination to a Christian identity. Distinctions do continue to exist—Asians are still Asian, males are still male—but such differences are seen within a christological matrix that exists between the believer and Christ and that believers have with each other. I may be a short-redhead-Caucasian-male-Aussie, but I am above all "in Christ";

that is what singularly determines who I am and how I value you as someone else who is "in Christ."

"I Do Not Permit a Woman to Teach" ... But Why? (1 Timothy 2:11–15)

> [11]A womanshould learn in quietness and full submission. [12]I do not permit a woman to teach or to assume authority over a man; she must be quiet. [13]For Adam was formed first, then Eve. [14]And Adam was not the one deceived; it was the woman who was deceived and became a sinner. [15]But women will be saved through childbearing—if they continue in faith, love and holiness with propriety.

Now we enter endgame. I used to think that this verse taught that women cannot teach or preach to men because they were second in line in the order of creation and they are inherently naïve and gullible. At the same time, there is a real prohibition here that needs to be taken seriously and not conveniently wiped aside. Let's keep in mind that on this matter prejudices operate in both spheres. Many Christians have been too accommodating toward a cultural trend that is explicitly opposed to Christian values (like radical feminism) or too willing to follow tradition even when that tradition is completely unbiblical in its assertions (like the view that women are inferior to men). At the same time the restriction here is real, it is not embarrassing, it is not an addition by a later disciple of Paul who did not share his master's liberal view of women, and it is part of the inspired teaching of Scripture. Nonetheless, many godly and gifted Christians have violently different opinions on what Paul meant and how it applies today.

Some Christians maintain that Paul's argument here is rooted in the order of creation ("for Adam was formed first"), so it is not indebted to the cultural circumstance or the historical situation in Ephesus and the argument is therefore universally applicable. The problem here is twofold. First, as I've noted earlier, Paul also appeals to creation in 1 Corinthians 11:3–16 in order to establish that women should wear head coverings. Yet all commentators who have done a basic course in hermeneutics acknowledge that the issue of head coverings is culturally restricted to the Greco-Roman environment of Corinth. Head coverings held certain connotations in that context that are not held everywhere. The transcultural application of 11:3–16 is that women should respect their respective heads just as men should respect their respective heads. Thus the appeal to the order of creation in 1 Timothy 2:13 does not require that the proscription about women teaching men must be uniformly applicable to all Christians at all times, since a broader principle may be what we are meant to take away. William Mounce concedes that "the context thus limits the universal application to some extent," since elsewhere women did teach (Acts 18:26; Col. 3:16; 2 Tim. 1:5; 3:15; Titus 2:3–4).[21]

Second, I am cautious about explaining this text in light of hypothetical reconstructions of the context, such as postulating the existence of a feminist verve in the Artemis cult in Ephesus and the entrance of Gnosticism into the church as the foil on which Paul's restrictions must be understood.[22] We should privilege the canonical text and its literary context; yet if we do so, we will observe that there are textual indicators that the heresy circulating in Ephesus did introduce aberrant views concerning women and their roles (see 1 Tim. 2:9–11, 15; 4:1–4; 5:11–16).[23]

As to the complementarian and egalitarian application of this text, I am going to try to thread an exegetical needle between them. I think it is worth pointing out that complementarians themselves qualify or tone down the full implications of their view, and herein is the weakness of their position. For example, some complementarians allow a woman to teach men indirectly through books, radio, and websites but will not permit them to teach men in person. A woman can write a commentary on Hebrews to be read by men but cannot preach or teach men on Hebrews. A woman can be president, a prime minister, a CEO, a general, or a police officer, but she cannot serve as a pastor. A woman can teach men French or piano lessons but not the Bible or theology. A woman can teach Bible and doctrine to unbelieving men but not to Christian men. The problem I have here is that some complementarians appeal to Genesis and the order of creation to show that it is inherently wrong for a woman to be in a position of authority over a man, and yet they only apply that restriction to church life or Sunday worship. But that is like saying that it is okay for someone to commit adultery as long as they do not do it on Sunday or in the church auditorium. Or it is like saying that it is okay to commit adultery as long as you do it with an unbeliever. If it is such a clear violation of God's ordering of creation for a woman to have authority over a man, then this should apply to all spheres of life whether it is business, government, politics, civil service, or church because God is sovereign over all institutions, and all of life is lived before God and under God.

At the same time, I have a bone to pick with the egalitarians since Paul does restrict women from teaching here, and it is at least *partly* because they are women that he does so. Paul gives a clear instance where it is desirable and necessary to prohibit women from teaching men. Even if one believes that the prohibition is tied to the situation in Ephesus, we should be prepared to use the same prohibition when similar situations arise.[24] Sending a lead female church planter in the Middle East is not going to get a lot of traction as several missionary friends have told me. Furthermore, if we think that the context of Paul's prohibition was partly driven by the sexual revolution of the first century,[25] then perhaps the sexual revolution of the 1960s–90s could lend warrant to a similar prohibition being used more commonly today. It is food for thought.

To get things going, let's get some cultural bearings by digging into Greco-Roman culture a bit. Attitudes toward women in the ancient world were very different to attitudes toward women in the modern Western world. What is more, attitudes, laws, rights, and expectations concerning women that differed between Jewish, Greek, and Roman contexts as well. So it will be helpful, then, if we understand some of the historical and cultural backgrounds to Paul's teaching about women and wives before we briefly delve into 1 Timothy 2:11–15. I cannot be exhaustive here since women in the ancient world is a huge topic, but I will point to three particular areas that impact how women were viewed in the world of the Pauline churches. I will focus on households, honor/shame, and the "new" Roman women.

First, we must situate the discussions about women in relation to the structure of households in Greco-Roman society. In the major cities of the Roman world, households were the basic living unit of the population. A household usually consisted of a head male, immediate family such as wives and children, extended relatives, slaves, freedmen, tenants, servants, sometimes business associates, and other retainers and dependents. The household provided security, identity, protection, and honor to its members. In many cases these households provided the physical location for house churches to gather together to pray, worship, and share communal meals (see Rom. 16:5; 1 Cor. 16:19; Col. 4:15; Philem. 2).

Women were often charged with running a household, where there was a network of relationships and expectations concerning the maintenance of the order and honor of the household. These expectations and obligations were usually expressed in "household codes," which go back as far as Aristotle. Similar household codes are found in the New Testament, especially in Paul's letters about the appropriate relationships between husbands and wives, masters and slaves, and parents and children (see Eph. 5:21–6:9; Col. 3:18–4:1; Titus 2:1–10).[26] It is notable that most of Paul's teachings about women are addressed to churches located in the major Roman cities of the Hellenistic world, where issues about conduct and conflict in households were a genuine question. The Christian household codes concern how the lordship of Jesus Christ over a community is to be lived out before the pagan world around them.

While these codes are undoubtedly patriarchal,[27] they express that patriarchy in light of mutual obligations of honor and love and they clearly censure abuses of authority. They were a necessary way of stabilizing a new religious movement that was regarded as politically subversive and socially offensive to cultural elites and civic powers. The Pauline household codes are not a reaffirmation of the status quo of pagan ethics or a mandate for social revolution; rather, they concern the authority of the Lord over the household of faith and the mutual obligations that follow from the subordination of all authority under the Lord. In a nutshell, it is the application of the principle of Colossians 3:17 to household life: "And whatever you do, whether in word or deed, do it all in the name of the Lord Jesus."[28] The thing to take away is that the makeup of households affected the leadership structures of some house churches, and biblical household codes were also influenced by cultural expectations for conduct within these households.[29]

Second, people of antiquity lived in an honor and shame culture. Honor was the public acknowledgment of one's worth dependent on the qualities that one embodied and the behavior valued by a certain group. Honor can be either ascribed by gender, social rank, and noble birth or else acquired through social advancement in public accomplishments and by excelling over others. Honor was a limited commodity in ancient societies, and it was attained through social competition and by avoiding disgrace.

For women honor was determined by the virtues of chastity and modesty. While maintaining honor and gaining honor was a chief aim of social interaction in the public sphere, Paul can tell the Romans: "Be devoted to one another in love. Honor one another above yourselves" (Rom. 12:10). They are not to play the honor game within the network of Christian relationships, which is why we find constant injunctions against rivalry and selfish ambition (2 Cor. 12:20; Gal. 5:20; Phil. 1:17; 2:3). You will not find Aristotle or Cicero advocating the virtue of humility since it was tantamount to self-debasement. Humility was for slaves, but Paul makes it the quintessential criteria for Christlikeness (Phil. 2:3, 5–11; Eph. 4:2; Col. 3:12). Relationships between husbands and wives must be understood in light of this honor-driven society where there was an obligation on husbands and wives to uphold each other's honor.[30]

Third, women in Greco-Roman society had mixed fortunes in their rights and treatments. Roman women enjoyed more freedom than their Greek counterparts, but both were relatively secluded from society except those who had to earn a living and were forced to work in the marketplace. Marriages were arranged and women were at the whim of the *patria potestas* or head of the household. Under Augustus a woman had the right to take legal action against a guardian whose actions toward her were deemed unreasonable. Under Claudius, guardianship of freeborn women was abolished, but not for freedwomen or ex-slaves.[31] Additionally, Bruce Winter has pointed out that there was a sexual revolution taking place in the first century, and many well-to-do women of the upper classes had taken to acting promiscuously. These "new Roman wives" dressed in such a way as to indicate that they were sexually avail-

able. These upper class women were clad in provocative dress, acted
with a lack of decorum, and departed radically from the image of
modesty that epitomized the traditional roles for wives and widows.[32] Some of the problems that Paul confronted may stem from
this environment.

To put the passage in context, 1 Timothy 2:8–15 concerns the
behavior and candor of men and women in public worship. Almost
every word and phrase is contested in this passage, but I will identify here two main issues on which an interpretation depends. First,
there is the character of the Ephesian heresy and its relation to the
women in Ephesus and the possibility that the situation is reflected
in the instructions given in these verses. Is Paul's remark a piece
of general instruction that is rooted in the order of creation and is
universally applicable, or are his instructions occasioned and driven
by the situation in Ephesus? A second issue is the meaning of the
words "teach" (*didaskō*) and "assume authority" (*authenteō*) in 1
Timothy 2:12. Do they mean two actions or one single action? Are
they positive ("don't teach from the position of elder") or negative
("don't teach heresy and domineer")?

What is certain is that in 1 and 2 Timothy teaching is usually
related to the office of overseer/elder since an overseer is to be able
to teach (1 Tim. 3:2; 5:17) and teaching is part of Timothy's charge
(4:11; 6:2; 2 Tim. 4:2). In addition, the beginning of 1 Timothy
2 has numerous couplets of synonymous ideas, such as "kings and
all those in authority," "peaceful and quiet lives," "godliness and
holiness" (v. 2), "this is good, and pleases God" (v. 3), "saved and . . .
come to a knowledge of the truth" (v. 4), "a herald and an apostle,"
"I am telling the truth, I am not lying" (v. 7), "anger or disputing"
(v. 8), "decency and propriety" (v. 9), and "quietness and full submission" (v. 11). Given that context, it is probable that "to teach"
and "to assume authority" are roughly approximate and refer to

something like "exercising authority through teaching." Does this teaching-authority refer to the positive exposition of Christian instruction, or does it refer to a negative thing like propagating heresy and domineering? Here are the options:

Positive

> Translation: I do not permit a woman to teach and *thus* to exercise authority over a man.
>
> Explanation: A prohibition of teaching doctrine to men from a legitimate position of Christian authority like the office of elder.
>
> Rationale: It violates the God-given order of creation.

Negative

> Translation: I do not permit a woman by *false* teaching to dominate a man.
>
> Explanation: A prohibition of teaching false doctrine as means to the usurpation of authority over men.
>
> Rationale: Women were propagating heresy with a view to gaining authority over men.

I am going to opt for the negative interpretation that Paul restricts women from teaching from the position of elder and teaching the elders because the views that they are disseminating are bound up with the heresy he is repudiating in 1 Timothy, and because their conduct is having adverse effects on the elders, husbands, and the congregation in general in Ephesus.

I find this position defensible and plausible because, first, in terms of the cultural context, the advent of the "new Roman women" in cities like Ephesus meant that some females of the upper echelons of society were determined to remain unencumbered by children, they aspired for the sexual freedoms of men, they threw off apparel symbolizing modesty and chastity, and they were brazenly outspoken in public forums. This kind of behavior finds a relatively neat home in the Pastorals with exhortations about learning in quietness, submissiveness, and modesty for women (1 Tim. 2:9–11).

Second, the false teaching encouraged asceticism (1 Tim. 4:3) and promoted endless genealogies, myths, and speculations about creation (1:3–4; 4:4, 7; 2 Tim. 4:4; cf. Titus 1:14), and it probably creatively tinkered with the story of Eve as well (1 Tim. 2:13–15). References to the prohibition of marriage and abstaining from certain foods (4:3) might reflect an attempt to return to the manner of life back in the garden of Eden before the fall. Some women were trying to follow a pattern of life based on certain myths about Genesis.[33] Like all great heresies there is a rewriting of the creation story and consequently a redefinition of salvation and a rehash of the relationship between men and women. When this is combined with an unrestrained spiritual enthusiasm that collapses the hope for the future age into present realities (2 Tim. 2:18), then you have a recipe for apostasy, divorce, and the breaking down of church order.

In the reference to women being "saved through childbearing" in 1 Timothy 2:15, Paul cannot be saying that a woman's salvation is dependent on her experience of having a baby travel down the birth canal. Nor is Paul saying that no Christian woman will ever die in childbirth because we know that some Christian women have died and do die in labor. Nor can Paul be speaking cryptically that a woman's salvation is contingent on her accepting the validity of patriarchal structures. None of that makes sense to me. Most likely, this verse is an attack on the heresy that maintained the opposite view, namely, that women are saved by not experiencing childbirth (for Eve was childless prior to the fall). Being childless through abstinence or abortion would also free up progressive wives to become women of leisure along the lines of the new bourgeois Roman wives. Paul urges women to embrace their identity precisely as Christian women instead of finding liberty in the heresy. Paul wants women to continue in faith, love, and holiness as the condition of salvation.[34] Furthermore, if we see traces of the heresy lying behind verse 15, why not a response to it in verses 12–14 as well? By drawing attention to Eve's role in the fall (v. 14) and her deference to Adam by divine design (v. 13), Paul is cutting the legs out from underneath the heresy that some women were advocating. The content of this heresy was something along the lines of a rewriting of the creation story that sought to subordinate their husbands or key church leaders beneath their own authority.

Third, Paul's use of *authenteō* ("to assume authority") probably has a negative connotation, given its usage in other literature and from the context here in particular.[35] John Chrysostom advised husbands: "Do not be despotic or domineer [*authentei*] the wife."[36] While *didaskō* for "to teach" usually has a positive meaning, there are negative uses of cognate words for teaching in 1 Timothy 4:1 and 6:3 in relation to unsound doctrine. Since the two words go together, a double negative meaning seems to fit best, namely, false teaching + domineering.

Paul does not want women dominating by propounding false doctrine in the Ephesian house churches. Paul is writing to a situation where certain well-to-do women, riding the cultural wave of feminine liberation, are trying to assume aggressively the mantle of leadership before they have properly learned the apostolic faith, and while they have come under the influence of false teachers who are rewriting the creation story to suit the inclinations of the new Roman women.[37] Paul won't stand for it.

That means that Paul's remarks here should be situated in a context of dissent from cultural norms for women, familial discord, and false teaching about gender and creation. It is rooted in a particular context, and we cannot just pick up and paste it into the twenty-first century without reflecting on when and where such prohibitions apply to us. I do not think Paul intends a once for all prohibition of women teaching men or leading in any kind of ministry. Paul wants women to learn and to avoid being deceived precisely because they are vital to the corporate teaching ministry of the churches. But there are definitely situations when women should not teach and when women should not lead.

That said, let me emphasize that my conclusion here is based on my reconstruction of the heresy as it relates to the women in Ephesus and my understanding of the connotations of the words for "teach" and "authority" in 1 Timothy 2:12 as negative—both of which are contestable. I invite my readers to be good Bereans and to investigate my hypothesis against Scripture itself (Acts 17:11) and to test all things and to hold fast to that which is good (1 Thess. 5:21).[38]

Conclusion

To wrap things up, I am not a full-on feminist because I think that it is somewhat anachronistic to suppose that Jesus and Paul were feminists in the modern sense of the term. Paul's ministry gave women a great amount of freedom and responsibility, but it still operated within a loving expression of patriarchy as is evident from the household codes. The relationship between husbands and wives as espoused in Ephesians and Colossians shows that husbandly headship has nothing to do with chauvinism and misogyny. There is also a real prohibition in 1 Timothy 2:11–15 that must be taken seriously, even when contextualized, and it cannot be easily swept aside as many commentators inadvertently do. Judith Gundry-Volf draws this apt conclusion:

> In sum, Paul seems to affirm *both* equality of status and roles of women and men in Christ *and* women's subordinate or secondary place. He appears to think that sometimes the difference between male and female is to be expressed in patriarchal conventions and that sometimes these conventions should be transcended or laid aside.[39]

However, I do not consider myself a complementarian because I have had to bow my knee to the biblical evidence that I think shows that women did teach men in the early church. The existence of women benefactors, prophets, deacons, and household leaders is a probable indicator that in some places, women were involved in the leadership structures of certain churches. The apostle Paul would roll over in his grave if he knew that Christians were treating his commandments like rabbinic case law and were compiling huge lists of things women can and cannot do.

I do not know what the middle ground is called, who holds it, or where it even is, but I have reached the point where I do not want to be pigeon-holed into either camp. I do not profess to have complete clarity on every exegetical issue, but personally I would rather listen to a sermon by a gifted woman than a sermon by an ungifted man. I have reservations about women occupying the senior roles of bishop or senior pastor since male headship still seems normative to me and more missionary contexts seem conducive to limiting women's roles in some instances. For ecumenical reasons too, I also have reservations about female ordination to the highest offices since this creates barriers with other ecclesial communities, but I recognize the authority of Scripture over any council, confession, or magisterium. As a husband and a father I do my best to lead and nurture my family, and as a Christian professor I do my utmost to empower and equip my female students to serve our common Lord in whatever way they feel led to do so and wish them every blessing and encouragement that I can offer them.

Paul Barnett offers a conservative but fairly inclusive view of women in ministry beyond the office of "senior pastor." He writes:

> If women prayed and prophesied in the churches, if they were encouraged to learn—as they are in this passage, if the older taught the younger, if they worked alongside Paul in the work of evangelism—then there is no good reason of exegesis or hermeneutics which would limit their ministries in those and related areas today. If 1 Tim. 2:11–15 restricts women from becoming the senior teacher to the family-congregation there appears to be no reason why they should be prevented from the whole range of pastoral, didactic or sacramental ministry under the leadership of the senior teacher in a team or in their own right in specialist, single sex congregations.[40]

What is more, I consider this whole debate a second order matter. First order doctrines are those which are essential and non-negotiable in the Christian belief mosaic, such as the Trinity, the inspiration of the Scriptures, the atonement, Christ's resurrection, Christ's return, and salvation by grace through faith—things without which one cannot be a Christian. Second order doctrines are those such as baptism, church government, or one's view of end-times theology, and other related matters that are indeed important for faith and the life of the church but are not ultimately obstructive for Christian unity. Third order doctrines are those that are *adiaphora* or matters of indifference, such as whether Christians can drink alcohol, whether should they homeschool their children, what Bible translations should they use, and the like. I submit that women in ministry is a second order doctrine insofar as it affects the life and direction of a church, but it is not the issue that separates the good guys from the bad guys. Churches and denominations can and should take a stand on these issues, yet recognize that it is not a matter of Christian faith and order that is at stake.

When I was engaged in doctoral studies, I met a lady who was a feminist of a particularly aggressive variety. I set out to ask her (provoke her really) about her understanding of 1 Timothy 2:11–15. In reply she gave one of the most impressive expositions of the complementarian position that I have ever heard. Yet when I asked her how we would go about implementing that interpretation in the church, she gave me a look as if I had just offered her a pornographic magazine. She said, "But the guy who wrote that was just a sexist bigot, so who cares what he thinks?" She followed up with several derogatory remarks against me for even making the suggestion. This woman saw Scripture as a document of history and that its message was negotiable. But that is not true of most egalitarians that I know.

My point is that critics should not accuse egalitarians of trying to undermine biblical authority or equate them with radical feminism. Evangelical egalitarians remain in the tradition of an orthodox Christianity and possess a high regard for Scripture even if (like all of us) they occasionally fall prey to the cultural ethos of our time. At the same time, complementarians do not wake up every morning and conspire how to oppress and abuse women. Many of them are deeply concerned with protecting women from abuse and stemming the exploitation of women, and they wish to see women reach their highest potential in Christ even if their own patriarchal culture rather than Scripture has shaped their thinking at times. In a nutshell, egalitarians are not opposed to biblical authority and complementarians are not deliberate oppressors of women. When both sides concede as much, then perhaps the gender war will be over.

Epilogue: Who Is Ilse Fredrichsdorff?

Who in the world is Ilse Fredrichsdorff? I came across a story about her while reading Robert Yarbrough's excellent book *The Salvation-Historical Fallacy*, where he refers to a quote that mentions her in the preface of a book by M. Albertz on *Die Botschaft des Neuen Testament* (*The Message of the New Testament*), written in Germany just after the World War II.[41] The citation reads:

This book is dedicated to the young brethren of the Confessing Church. I was united with them in my office as leader of the Office of Theological Examination of the Confessing Church in Berlin-Brandenburg. I was all the closer to these brethren, whose status was illegal from the start, in that performance of my ministry resulted in the loss of my freedom as well as my ordination, withdrawn by a bogus ecclesiastical authority. The book's dedication bears two names [one is Erich Klapproth, the other is Ilse Fredrichsdorff].... When the church began she [Ilse Fredrichsdorff] was a young girl belonging to the Confessing Church congregation Nicolai-Melanchthon in Spandau. Through our congregation she came to take up theological study. She studied in our theological college and in Basel with Karl Barth. She became curate of the only truly evangelical confessional school that could be established under the Third Reich, the school for non-Aryan Christian children who were no longer permitted to attend the public school. During the war she remained in congregations northeast of Berlin, in that region where the last battle prior to Berlin was waged. She was so much in demand for her pastoral skills that the major of the troop emplacements behind which lay the villages she served repeatedly requested her aid among the troops. Later she led the displaced congregations with the word of God, went back to the hunger zone as much as possible, and, after she had buried hundreds of the thousands who perished, succumbed herself to starvation.

That's an amazing story of really taking up your cross and serving Christ. What do you say to that kind of story?[42] Now if you are a consistent complementarian, you would be forced to say something like, "Ilse Fredrichsdorff was the prime example of everything that a woman should not be, a pastor. She may have done some good given the extreme circumstances of her time, but ultimately her pastoral work did not bring glory to God because she undertook Christian ministry in direct disobedience to God's command." Now I am conscious of the fact that saying, "Look, there is a really nice person, who did some nice things for God, who even died while serving God, so God must approve of her," is not a good argument. That is because you could make the same argument about a lesbian Episcopalian or a transgendered Unitarian who have done some brave things in tough times. Sentimentality is not the yardstick for biblical truth.

That said, the problem is that women like Ilse Fredrichsdorff are not exceptions that prove the rule; rather, they stand in a long line of women from the apostolic age across church history who have served God in areas such as leading communities and teaching God's Word to others. Dozens of examples could be given, and I mention here only a few.

- During the Reformation, Katherine Zell was perhaps the most active and headstrong of all of the Reformers' wives, having her own ministry to religious refugees and even presiding over a funeral.
- The founder of Methodism, John Wesley, and the Puritan Matthew Poole both permitted women to speak in gathered

Christian assemblies if they felt led by the Spirit, and from all accounts many women did.

- There was the well-known woman preacher Anne Hutchinson in colonial New England.
- Missionary women like Anne Judson in Burma, Amy Carmichael in India, or Gladys Aylward in China all served the cause of the gospel in foreign lands.
- Women preachers were active in the abolitionist movement in the nineteenth century and in the suffragette movement of the twentieth century.
- We might also remember the evangelistic work of Catherine Booth, the cofounder of the Salvation Army with her husband, William Booth.

If I had time, I would love to document the work of indigenous women in Africa, Asia, and South America, who have faithfully served God in positions of leadership and as proclaimers of the gospel of Jesus Christ.

What are we to do with these women? Can we blot out their names from the annals of church history? Can we use them as negative examples of what women should not be? Can we praise their intentions while frowning on their ministry? We are confronted with such women, in our past and even in our present, and they have always been a thorny enigma in the theological sides of those who would prohibit women from all forms of leadership and from teaching in the church. A more inclusive and more biblical approach to Christian ministry will allow us to embrace such women as fellow soldiers of Christ and partners in the gospel.

Further Reading

There is a vast amount of literature written on the subject of Paul and women. The following studies are ones that I've found particularly helpful over the years.

Beacon Spencer, Aida. *Beyond the Curse: Women and the Call to Ministry*. Nashville: Nelson, 1985.

Blomberg, Craig L. "Neither Hierarchicalist nor Egalitarian: Gender Roles in Paul." Pages 283–326 in *Paul and His Theology*, ed. Stanley E. Porter. Leiden: Brill, 2006.

———, ed. *Two Views on Women in Ministry*. Grand Rapids: Zondervan, 2001.

Cohick, Lynn. *Women in the World of the Earliest Christians: Illuminating Ancient Ways of Life*. Grand Rapids: Baker, 2009.

DeYoung, James. *Women in Ministry: Neither Egalitarian Nor Complementarian: A New Approach to an Old Problem*. Eugene, OR: Cascade, 2010.

Gundry, Patricia. *Neither Slave Nor Free: Helping Women Answer the Call to Church Leadership*. San Francisco: Harper & Row, 1990.

Husbands, Mark A., and Timothy Larsen, eds. *Women, Ministry, and the Gospel: Exploring New Paradigms*. Downers Grove, IL: InterVarsity Press, 2007.

Keener, Craig S. *Paul, Women and Wives: Marriage and Women's Ministry in the Letters of Paul*. Peabody, MA: Hendrickson, 1992.

Köstenberger, Andreas. "Women in the Pauline Mission." Pages 221–47 in *The Gospel for the Nations: Perspectives on Paul's Mission*, eds. Peter G. Bolt and Mark D. Thompson. Leicester, UK.: Apollos, 2000.

————. *Studies on John and Gender: A Decade of Scholarship.* New York: Peter Lang, 2001.

McKnight, Scot. *Junias is Not Alone.* Patheos: Patheos.com, 2011.

Perriman, Andrew. *Speaking of Women: Interpreting Paul.* Leicester, UK: Apollos, 1998.

Sumner, Sarah. *Men and Women in the Church.* Downers Grove, IL: InterVarsity Press, 2003.

Witherington, Ben, III. *Women in the Ministry of Jesus: A Study of Jesus' Attitudes towards Women and Their Roles as Reflected in His Earthly Life.* Cambridge: Cambridge University Press, 1984.

————. *Women in the Earliest Churches.* Cambridge: Cambridge University Press, 1988.

About the Author

Dr. Michael F. Bird (PhD, University of Queensland) is Lecturer in Theology and Bible at Crossway College in Brisbane, Australia. He is the author of over ten books, including *The Saving Righteousness of God*, *A Bird's Eye-View of Paul*, and *Colossians and Philemon*. Michael is a prolific co-blogger of Euangelion (with Joel Willitts), one of the top fifty biblical-theological blogs (http://euangelizomai .blogspot.com/). He lives in Brisbane, Australia, with his wife, Naomi, and their four children.

Notes

1. John R. Rice, *Bobbed Hair, Bossy Wives, and Women Preachers* (Wheaton, IL: Sword of the Lord, 1941).

2. Patricia Gundry, *Woman, Be Free!* (Grand Rapids: Zondervan, 1977).

3. Stanley E. Gundry, "From *Bobbed Hair, Bossy Wives, and Women Preachers* to *Woman Be Free,*" *CBE International*. www.cbeinternational.org/?q=content/bobbed-hair-bossy-wives-and-women-preachers. Cited 12 Jan 2012.

4. See Alan F. Johnson, ed., *How I Changed My Mind about Women in Leadership* (Grand Rapids: Zondervan, 2010).

5. See further Ben Witherington III, *Romans: A Socio-Rhetorical Commentary* (Grand Rapids: Eerdmans, 2004), 377–95; and his earlier works: *Women in the Ministry of Jesus: A Study of Jesus' Attitude to Women and Their Roles as Reflected in His Earthly Life* (Cambridge: Cambridge University Press, 1984); idem, *Women and the Genesis of Early Christianity* (Cambridge: Cambridge University Press, 1990).

6. I should also point out that the T4G 2008 conference seemed to have rectified the problem by booking a larger facility able to accommodate a larger group and women were welcomed to attend, but still, the treatment of women at T4G 2006 was not particularly encouraging to those of us who believe that women are crucial to the advance of the gospel.

7. But see in counterpoint Benjamin L. Merkle, "Paul's Arguments from Creation in 1 Corinthians 11:8–9 and 1 Timothy 2:13–14: An Apparent Inconsistency Answered," *JETS* 49 (2006): 527–48. Merkle suggests that 1 Cor. 11:8–9 uses the creation argument *indirectly*, while 1 Tim. 2:13–14 employs it *directly*, rendering the latter command transcultural. My problem is that direct or indirect, Paul still uses creation imagery to argue for what is essentially a culturally specific matter in 1 Cor. 11:8–9, which remains analogous to the type of argument used in 1 Tim. 2:13–14.

8. Two representative publications are Ronald W. Pierce, Rebecca Merrill Groothuis, and Gordon D. Fee, eds., *Discovering Biblical Equality: Complementarity without Hierarchy* (Downers Grove, IL: InterVarsity Press, 2005), and John Piper and Wayne Grudem, eds., *Recovering Biblical Manhood and Womanhood: A Response to Evangelical Feminism* (Wheaton, IL: Crossway, 1991).

9. This table is an adaptation from a handout by Gerry Breshears and Debbie Dodd distributed at the annual meeting of the Evangelical Theological Society in Philadelphia, 2005.

10. Cf., e.g., Craig L. Blomberg, *1 Corinthians* (NIVAC; Grand Rapids: Zondervan, 1994), 208–10; Ben Witherington III, *Conflict and Community in Corinth: A Socio-Rhetorical Commentary on 1 and 2 Corinthians* (Grand Rapids: Eerdmans, 1995), 237–38; Richard B. Hays, *First Corinthians* (Interpretation; Louisville: Westminster John Knox, 1997), 184; Anthony C. Thiselton, *The First Epistle to the Corinthians* (NIGTC; Grand Rapids: Eerdmans, 2000), 812–26; Craig S. Keener, *1–2 Corinthians* (NCBC; Cambridge: Cambridge University Press, 2005), 92–93.

11. I think that the ESV is right on 1 Cor. 11:3 to translate *anēr* as "husband" and *gynaikos* as "wife" since it was only married women who were expected to wear head coverings in Roman culture.

12. That it is the relationship between men and women and not only the women's practice of wearing head coverings that is corrected, see Jerome Murphy-O'Connor, "Sex and Logic in 1 Cor 11:2–16," *CBQ* 92 (1980): 482–500.

13. Judith Gundry-Volf, "Gender and Creation in 1 Cor 11:2–16: A Study in Paul's Theological Method," in *Evangelium, Schriftauslegung, Kirche*, eds.J. Ådna, S. Hafemann, and O. Hofius (FS Peter Stuhlmacher; Göttingen: Vandenhoeck & Ruprecht, 1997), 151–71.

14. Roy E. Ciampa and Brian S. Rosner, *The First Letter to the Corinthians* (PNTC; Grand Rapids: Eerdmans, 2010), 503.

15. Ibid., 504.

16. The most thorough argument for this position is Philip B. Payne, *Man and Woman, One in Christ: An Exegetical and Theological Study of Paul's Letters* (Grand Rapids: Zondervan, 2009), 217–67.

17. See helpful discussions of the evidence in Thiselton, *First Epistle to the Corinthians*,1150–61; David E. Garland, *1 Corinthians* (BECNT; Grand Rapids: Baker, 2003), 667–73.

18. For further discussion see Alan Padgett, *As Christ Submits to the Church: A Biblical Understanding of Leadership and Mutual Submission* (Grand Rapids: Baker Academic, 2011).

19. Richard Bauckham, *Gospel Women: Studies in the Named Women of the Gospels* (Grand Rapids: Eerdmans, 2002), 180.

20. Eldon J. Epp, *Junia: The First Woman Apostle* (Minneapolis: Fortress, 2005), 81.

21. William D. Mounce, *Pastoral Epistles* (WBC; Nashville: Nelson, 2000), 123.

22. This theory has been thoroughly discredited by Steven M. Baugh, "A Foreign World: Ephesus in the First Century," in *Women in the Church: A Fresh Analysis of 1 Timothy 2:9–15* (ed. Andreas Köstenberger, Thomas R. Schreiner, and H. Scott Baldwin; Grand Rapids: Baker, 1995), 13–52.

23. On the false teaching in Ephesus that is represented in the Pastoral Epistles see 1 Timothy 1:3–7, 18–20; 4:1–10; 6:2–10, 20–21 and 2 Timothy 2:14–26; 3:1–9, 4:1–5. For an overview of methodology in locating the heresy and identifying its basic contours see Ben Witherington III, *Letters and Homilies for Hellenized Christians—Volume 1: A Socio-Rhetorical Commentary on Titus, 1–2 Timothy and 1–3 John* (Nottingham: Apollos, 2006), 341–47.

24. Philip H. Towner, *The Letters to Timothy and Titus* (NICNT; Grand Rapids: Eerdmans, 2006), 239.

25. Bruce W. Winter, *Roman Wives, Roman Widows: The Appearance of New Women and the Pauline Communities* (Grand Rapids: Eerdmans, 2003), 1–74, 173–211.

26. Cf. also 1 Tim. 2:1–15; 6:1–2, 17–19; 1 Pet. 2:18–3:7.

27. According to Wayne A. Meeks (*The First Urban Christians: The Social World of the Apostle Paul* [New Haven, CT: Yale University Press, 1983], 76): "The head of the household by normal expectations of the society would exercise some authority over the group and would have some legal responsibility for it. The structure of the *oikos* [house] was hierarchical, and contemporary political and moral thought regarded the structure of superior and inferior roles as basic to the well-being of the whole society."

28. Michael F. Bird, *Colossians and Philemon* (NCCS; Eugene, OR: Cascade, 2009), 113–14.

29. Carolyn Osiek and Margaret Y. MacDonald, *A Woman's Place: House Churches in Earliest Christianity* (Minneapolis: Fortress, 2006), 144–63.

30. See further David deSilva, "Honor and Shame," in *Dictionary of New Testament Background* (ed. Craig A. Evans and Stanley E. Porter; Downers Grove, IL: InterVarsity Press, 2000), 518–22.

31. Thiselton, *The First Epistle to the Corinthians*, 802.

32. Winter, *Roman Wives, Roman Widows*, 97–120.

33. E. Schlarb, *Die gesunde Lehre: Häeresie und Wahrheit im Spiegel der Pastoralbriefe* (Marburg: N.G. Elwert, 1990), 83–133 (esp. 123–24).

34. See Stanley E. Porter, "What Does it Mean to be 'Saved by Childbirth' (1 Timothy 2.15)?" *JSNT* 49 (1993): 87–102.

35. BDAG, 150: "to assume a stance of independent authority, *give orders to, dictate to*" and JB: "tell a man what to do."

36. John Chrysostom, *Homilies on Colossians* 10.

37. Witherington, *Letters and Homilies for Hellenized Christians*,231.

38. I recommend students consult the commentaries by Towner, *Timothy and Titus*, 212–39; Mounce, *Pastoral Epistles*, 94–49; I Howard Marshall, *The Pastoral Epistles* (ICC: Edinburgh: T&T Clark, 1999), 452–71; and Andreas Köstenberger, "1 Timothy," *The Expositor's Bible Commentary: Ephesians—Philemon* (rev. ed.; ed. Tremper Longman and David E. Garland; Grand Rapids: Zondervan, 2006), 12:515–30, for a diverse survey of opinion.

39. Judith Gundry-Volf, "Paul on Women and Gender: A Comparison of Early Jewish Views," in *The Road from Damascus: The Impact of Paul's Conversion on his Life, Thought, and Ministry* (ed. Richard N. Longenecker; Grand Rapids: Eerdmans, 1997),186.

40. Paul Barnett, "Wives and Women's Ministry (1 Timothy 2:11–15)," *EvQ* 3 (1989): 237.

41. Robert W. Yarbrough, *The Salvation Historical Fallacy: Reassessing the History of New Testament Theology* (Leiden: Deo, 2004), 342 n. 9.

42. On the Internet, I did locate a reference to a thesis (in German) written about Ilse Fredrichsdorff, written by Renate Schatz-Hurschmann and called *Ein Frau ist immer im Dienst: Das Leben der Isle Fredrichsdorff* (*A Woman Is in the Ministry: The Life of Ilse Fredrichsdorff*).